SPIDERS AROUND THE WORLD

All About North American BLACK WIDOW SPIDERS

John Bankston

Mitchell Lane
PUBLISHERS
2001 SW 31st Avenue
Hallandale, FL 33009
www.mitchelllanepub.com

Little Mitchie

First Edition, 2025.

Author: John Bankston
Designer: Ed Morgan
Editor: Morgan Brody

Little Mitchie is an imprint of Mitchell Lane Publishers.

Title: All About North American Black Widow Spiders
Description: Hallandale, FL : Mitchell Lane Publishers, [2025]

Series: Spiders Around the World: North America
Library bound ISBN: 978-1-68020-933-4
eBook ISBN: 978-1-68020-944-0
Paperback ISBN: 979-8-89260-160-3

Photo credits: Shutterstock

Contents

The snake does not see the black widow spider. It doesn't see its web. That's too bad for the snake! The spider waits. The snake gets stuck in the web. The black widow bites. Its sharp fangs send **venom** into the snake. The snake dies. Now the black widow can eat for weeks.

Most spiders don't eat snakes. North American black widows do. They also like grasshoppers, flies, beetles, and mosquitoes. North American black widow spiders are the size of your fingernail. Yet they can kill much bigger **prey**. Black widows can also be eaten by praying mantises, alligator lizards, and blue mud wasps.

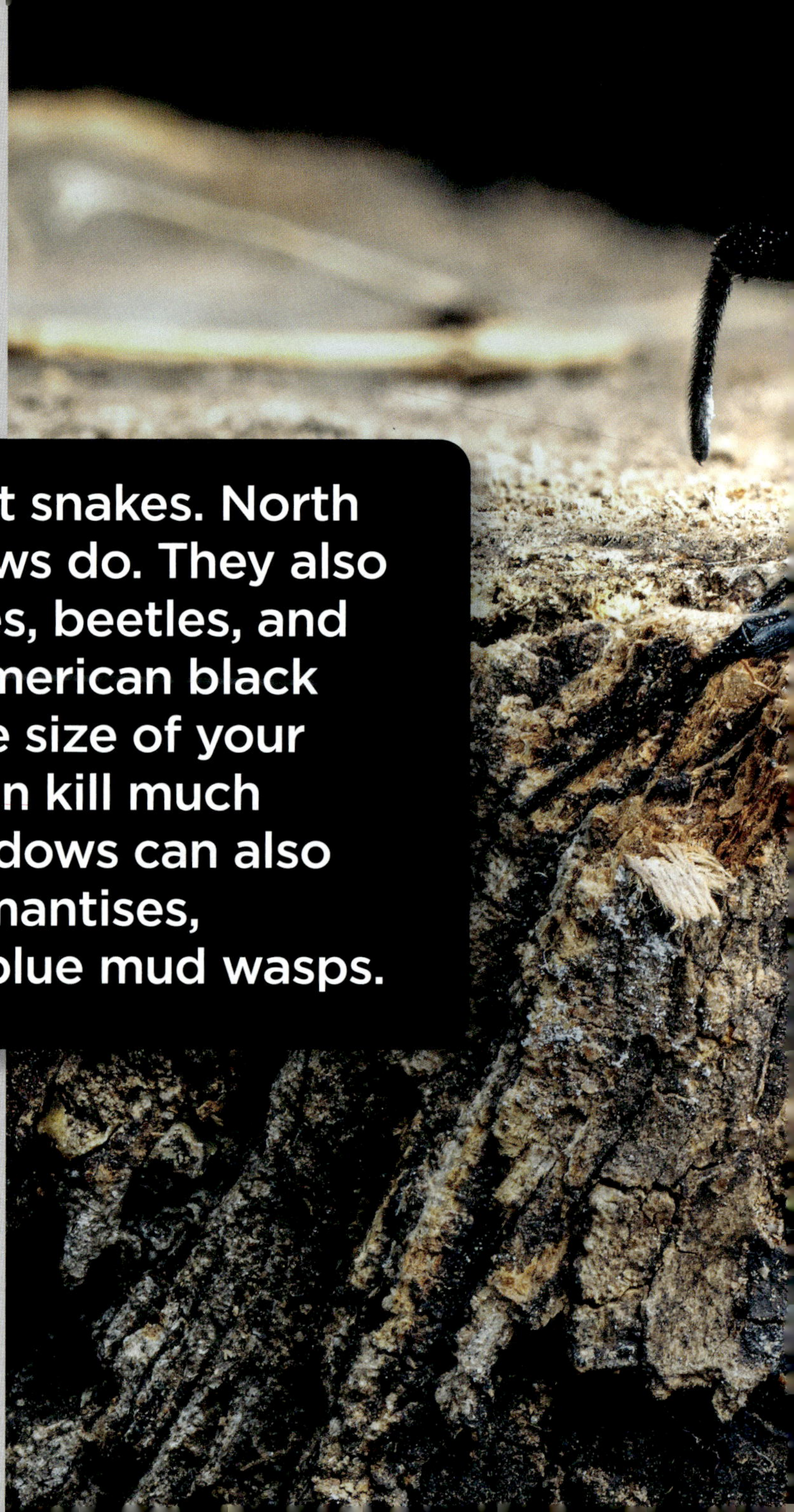

The black widow uses venom to kill. This venom is very strong. It is stronger than even a rattlesnake's venom. Their webs are also very tough. They can look messy. Black widows spin different types of webs.

These spiders are shiny black. They have a red mark on their **abdomen**. It looks like an hourglass or two triangles.

Females lay 200 eggs. They keep them in a sac on their web. It takes 20 days for them to hatch. The babies then live in a **cocoon** for a month.

Black widow females sometimes eat smaller males. That's why they are called black widows. Males have less venom. They only live a few months. Females can live three years.

Black widows live in wooded places. They like dark basements. They hide in gardens. They stay close to the ground.

A black widow bite feels like a pinprick. It can make you very sick. These spiders avoid people. They are also hard to spot. Keep an eye out. If you are ever bitten by a spider, get an adult's help right away! Spider bites can cost you an arm or a leg!

Never put your hands or feet somewhere without looking first. Black widows are great at hiding!

Where Do North American Black Widow Spiders Live?

The three species of black widows live across the United States and parts of Canada.

Interesting Facts

- North American black widows have been seen killing more snakes than any other spider. That includes the huge and scary looking tarantula!
- Bridge builders study black widow spider webs. That's because they are very thin and light but also very strong.
- Only female black widows bite people. Two-thousand people are bit in the U.S. every year.
- Black widows don't see well. Their web lets them know what's going on.
- They are comb-footed spiders. That means they have hair on two legs that look like a comb's teeth.

Parts of a North American Black Widow Spider

Spiders are **arachnids**. Their skeleton is outside of their body. Their head and **thorax** are fused. This part is called the cephalothorax.

Abdomen
The abdomen holds the silk glands. This is how it creates its web. It also holds its heart and guts. They have a red hourglass-shaped design on the underside of their body.

Legs
Its eight legs are on the cephalothorax. There are claws on the end of its legs.

Mouth
This is where its fangs are. It also has feelers nearby.

Glossary

abdomen (ab-DOE-men)
Place where the stomach is located

arachnids (a-rack-NIDS)
An eight-legged creature without antenna

cocoon (cuh-COON)
Case that protects arachnids before they are born

prey (pray)
Insect or other creature hunted for food

species (speesh-EEZs)
Living things that are very similar

thorax (thor-AX)
The middle part of the bod

venom (ven-OM)
A dangerous liquid that is injected by an animal

Further Reading

Culliford, Amy. *Black Widow Spider (Deadliest Animals).* St. Catharine's, Canada. Crabtree Books, 2021.

Gleisner, Jenna Lee. *Black Widows.* Minneapolis, MN : Bullfrog books, 2019.

On the Internet

This page shows you the many parts of a Black Widow:
https://www.enchantedlearning.com/subjects/arachnids/spider/Blackwidowprintout.shtml

Learn all about the Black Widow from National Geographic:
https://kids.nationalgeographic.com/animals/invertebrates/facts/black-widow#

Find out more from A to Z animals:
https://a-z-animals.com/animals/black-widow-spider/

Index